PORTFOLIOS:
ASSESSING LEARNING IN THE PRIMARY GRADES

by Marianne Lucas Lescher

NEA Professional Library
National Education Association
Washington, D.C.

The Author

Marianne Lucas Lescher is a special educator and core evaluation team chair at the Martha Jones School in Westwood, Massachusetts, and a doctoral candidate at Boston College in educational research and measurement. She has worked with alternative assessment strategies for 12 years.

Advisory Panel

David Bell
Professor of Education
Arkansas Tech University
Russellville, Arkansas

Geraldine Doswell
Retired Elementary School
  Counselor
Lawrenceville, New Jersey

Dana T. Elmore
Professor Emeritus
San Jose State University
San Jose, California

Martha Mitchell
Parent-Infant Coordinator
Zanesville City Schools
Zanesville, Ohio

Barbara J. Schram
Elementary Teacher (Pre K-2)
Delta Center Elementary School
Grand Ledge, Michigan

Lanita Sheffer
Kindergarten Teacher
Glen Loch Elementary School
Woodlands, Texas

Copyright © 1995
National Education Association of the United States

Printing History
First Printing: April 1995

ACID FREE
∞

Note

The opinions expressed herein should not be construed as representing the policy or position of the National Education Association. Materials published by the NEA Professional Library are intended to be discussion documents for educators who are concerned with specialized interests of the profession.

Library of Congress Cataloging-in-Publication Data

Lescher, Marianne Lucas.
    Portfolios: assessing learning in the primary grades / by
  Marianne Lucas Lesher.
      p. cm. — (What research says to the teacher)
  Includes bibliographical references (p. 38-40).
  ISBN 0-8106-1094-9
  1. Portfolios in education—United States. 2. Education, Primary—United States—Evaluation. 3. Language arts (Primary)—United States — Evaluation.   I.Title. II. Series.
LB1029.P67L47 1995
372.12'7 — dc20
                                              95-4295
                                                 CIP

Contents

Introduction 5
Literacy Assessment Portfolios Defined
And Described 5

Toward a New Theory for Assessing
Literacy Development 10

An Outdated Model of Assessment 11

*Discoveries About the Acquisition of
Language and Literacy* 12

Essential Components of
Portfolio Assessment 14
Observation and Anecdotal Records 15

Checklists 16

Work Samples 18

Formal Literacy Skill Assessments 19

Concepts About Literacy 20

Spelling and Phonetic Skill Development 21

Expressive Writing Proficiency .23

Oral Reading Fluency and Comprehension 24

Student Self-Assessments 25

Learning Logs 26

Survey Questions 26

Student Selection of Portfolio Entries 27

Conferences 27

Conferences with Students 27

Conferences with Peers 28

Conferences with Parents 28

Logs and Journals 29

PUTTING PORTFOLIO ASSESSMENT TO WORK 30

Creating an Environment that Supports
Portfolio Assessment 30

The Role of the Classroom Teacher 30

The Arrangement of the Daily Routine 31

The Physical Layout of the Classroom 31

Interpreting and Analyzing Portfolios 32

Communicating Student Growth and
Development to Parents 33

Taking the First Steps Toward
Portfolio Assessment 35

Bibliography 38

INTRODUCTION

As today's teachers reflect on student progress, they are interested in much more than isolated scores on standardized tests or the unit tests in textbooks. Such traditional assessment methods—which regrettably have often become ends in themselves—are just not enough anymore. Teachers need better assessments, ones that facilitate growth in many domains so that students can learn to think, reflect, analyze their own work, and solve problems independently.

Thus, teachers and researchers have been searching out new ways to assess student progress across multiple domains. Looking for new insights that enhance daily teaching practices, teachers have shown interest in learning-styles research and new assessment options. Of these alternative assessment strategies, portfolio assessment is one of the most potent. Many educators have embraced portfolio assessment because they believe it can:

- highlight process as well as product,
- value effort and improvement along with product, and
- continually engage students in self-reflection (Tierney, Carter, and Desai 1991).

Although this work focuses primarily on literacy assessment portfolios, you can adapt many of the ideas presented to your particular subject area.

LITERACY ASSESSMENT PORTFOLIOS DEFINED AND DESCRIBED

For a long time, portfolios have been used to assess and document progress in the arts. Photographers, artists, and writers commonly compile collections of their work to show how their talent and performance has grown and evolved. In much the same way, teachers are now assisting students to develop and analyze portfolios that document progress in learning to read and write. For additional information on the classroom use of portfolios, see *Student Portfolios*. (Grovenor et al. 1993).

Literacy assessment portfolios can take many forms, but at the root of all assessment portfolios are several key characteristics:

- Portfolios are *systematic collections* with contributions from both students and teachers (Tierney, Carter, and Desai 1991). Well beyond mere storehouses of completed work, portfolios include work that is carefully chosen to track the evolution of a student's skill, achievement, and progress and to exemplify the breadth and depth of the student's experience (Valencia 1990b).

- Portfolios are not stagnant entities. Instead, they *actively involve students* in creating, assessing, evaluating, and revising portfolio entries.

- The portfolio is not an aloof and exclusive preserve, either. It is a *joint responsibility and resource*. Collecting data and the assessment process overall is "a shared responsibility among teachers, students, parents and administrators" (Church 1991). As a result, the portfolio provides a basis for constant communication between and among the teachers, students, parents, and administrators involved (Graves and Sunstein 1992).

- Because portfolio assessment is *inextricably linked with instruction,* teachers must become adept in the use of portfolios to analyze student growth and progress. Only in this way can portfolio data be incorporated immediately into classroom practice, thereby continuing the cyclical nature of assessment and instruction as well as providing for the ever-evolving needs of students.

- Portfolios must be *multidimensional.* Since the processes of learning to read and write are very complex, assessments documenting progress in these areas must sample a wide range of cognitive processes, affective responses, and literacy activities (Valencia 1990b). In practice, this requirement means that portfolios must include a variety of types of indicators so that teachers, parents, administrators, and students can build a full, complete picture of literacy development (Valencia 1990b). The range should include various types of written responses to reading, written work in daily journals or logs, various pieces of writing reflecting different stages of completion, checklists, progress reports, classroom-based

Figure 1
Portfolios: Key Characteristics
Portfolios are purposeful collections of student work that tell the story of a student's efforts, progress, and achievement.

Systematic collection	• Both students and teachers contribute • Shows evolution of student's skills, achievement, and progress
Actively involves students	• Portfolios are not stagnant • Students participate in creating, assessing, evaluating, and revising portfolio entries.
Joint responsibilities and resources	• Collecting and assessing are shared among teachers, students, parents, and administrators • A basis for constant communication among teachers, students, parents, and administrators
Inextricably linked with instruction	• Portfolio data must be incorporated immediately into classroom practice • Assessment and instruction are cyclical
Multi-dimensional	• Must document progress in cognitive processes, affective responses, and subject matter activities • Can include written school work, journals or logs, assigned work at various stages of completion, checklists, projects, teacher's observations, and student self-evaluations.
Anchored in authenticity	• Real reading and writing • Purposeful activities • Projects

assessments, projects, teacher's observations and notes, and periodic student self-evaluations. The specific components included can be agreed upon as a school system, within one school, or on a teacher-by-teacher basis.

- The assessments and activities included within the portfolio must be *anchored in authenticity.* That is, they must involve real reading, real writing, and purposeful activities.

Portfolios, then, are purposeful collections of student work that tell the story of a student's efforts, progress, and achievement. An important aspect of the use of portfolios is that the student participates in selecting the portfolio's content, creating guidelines for the selection of content, establishing criteria for judging the merit of entries, and providing evidence of self-reflection (Arter and Spandel 1992).

This definition, which was developed by the Northwest Evaluation Association, supports the view that portfolio assessment must be "continuous, capture a rich array of what students know and can do, involve realistic contexts, communicate to students and others what is valued, portray the processes by which work is accomplished, and be integrated with instruction." The portfolio should also act as a "shifting, growing repository of developing processes and ideas" (Farr 1992). Yet another requirement is that portfolios be personally useful. To the student, they must constitute "reflective collections, revealing genuinely individual and personal responses" (Farr 1992).

Beyond these characteristic traits, portfolio forms vary widely. In some cases, separate reading and writing folders are created, and from them, a teacher and student will collaboratively select pieces of work that are the most reflective of the student's growth and progress. In other systems, evidence from several arenas is collected simultaneously. The portfolio may include student reading and writing samples, along with teacher-directed activities and assessments that provide a class profile by

Each student's portfolio is different because each student is different!

Figure 2
Portfolio Design Worksheet
Your student portfolios must answer at least four questions. Your team can use this worksheet to begin to design your student portfolios.

1. What needs to be assessed?

   _____
   _____
   _____
   _____

2. Who will be involved in the assessment process?

   _____
   _____
   _____
   _____

3. How will data be collected and analyzed?

   _____
   _____
   _____
   _____

4. What components will be included in the portfolio?
   - ☐ observational/anecdotal records
   - ☐ checklists
   - ☐ work samples
   - ☐ formal skill assessments
   - ☐ _____
   - ☐ _____
   - ☐ _____

   - ☐ informal skill assessments
   - ☐ student self-assessments
   - ☐ conference logs and records
   - ☐ various types of journals and learning logs
   - ☐ _____
   - ☐ _____

5. _____ ?

   _____
   _____
   _____

   (Add other questions that you think are important)

collecting the same type of data from each member of the class. Some portfolios include documentation in math, social studies, and science.

These variations are perfectly acceptable. It is the very nature of portfolios that they be flexible and evolving. They can be designed to accomplish myriad ends. They can be many things to many teachers and students. In fact, each student's portfolio is different because each student is different!

When portfolios are developed with these ideas in mind, they lead to three worthwhile ends. First, they "promote a richer and more sophisticated understanding" of student work and "reward rather than punish the essential things we try to place at the heart" of instruction: exploration and questioning, discussion, feedback, and revision. Second, in urging students to revise and refine, rather than give up, portfolios dispose students toward continuous effort and constant improvement. Third, portfolio assessment is intrinsically encouraging. It "takes the stance of an invitation to students: Can you show us your best work, so we can see what you know and what you can do—not just what you do not know and cannot do?" (Elbow 1991).

TOWARD A NEW THEORY FOR ASSESSING LITERACY DEVELOPMENT

Through a process of observation, reflection, and discovery, teachers and researchers together have conducted inquiries about the assessment of literacy development. In collaboration with researchers, teachers have discussed and pinpointed the positive and negative characteristics of their classrooms and schools. Researchers have spent time in classrooms observing and collecting data on the processes used to acquire literacy skills and fluency. These inquiries even extended to other countries. In nations where the literacy rate is far superior to that in the United States, data was collected on the methodologies and strategies used in early childhood education. Observers questioned and collected data on thousands of students, teachers, and classrooms (Clay 1991; Clay 1979; Fisher 1991; Graves and Sunstein 1992; Goodman, Goodman, and Hood 1989; Kemp 1987; Teale 1988; Valencia and Sulzby 1991).

This research on the assessment of children's progress toward literacy has led to some important new conclusions. Two in particular stand out. One has to do with the outdated assessment model that is prevalent in American schools. Another has to do with discoveries about how language and literacy are acquired.

An Outdated Model of Assessment

To many people, the words "assessment" and "testing" evoke the same image: rows of desks with students sitting silently working on paper-and-pencil tasks, perhaps filling in bubbles or circling responses to short questions concerning isolated snippets of information. This approach is still widely accepted and used. For instance, it permeates qualifying and entrance examinations, such as the Scholastic Aptitude Test (SAT).

A chief reason that the testing approach to assessment endures is that it seems to satisfy this country's insatiable enthusiasm for simple, bottom-line types of information. American consumers of information want assessment data reduced to very small, ostensibly easy-to-understand chunks that lend themselves to the reporting formats of newspapers and television. While the standardized test scores and reports do, in fact, have a place in today's schools, they must be taken as one piece of data in a picture of student progress that should include hundreds of pieces of data collected over many years.

Unfortunately, the notion that assessment is equivalent to testing has become part of the bedrock of our nation's schools. Teachers, parents, and community members have been led to believe that isolated numbers in reports received once or twice a year are true and complete indicators of student achievement. Many schools accordingly cling to their traditional notions of testing and continue to spend an inordinate amount of time and money on the purchase and development of tests, test administration and scoring, and on the reports that must be generated from the data collected.

This devotion to testing is far from cost-free. Our testing endeavors are often pursued at

Unfortunately, the notion that assessment is equivalent to testing has become part of the bedrock of our nation's schools.

the expense of structured opportunities for teachers to develop mechanisms for collecting more genuinely representative assessment data. Such information would lend real meaning to teachers' daily practices and more truly reflect individual students' progress.

Discoveries About the Acquisition of Language and Literacy

The other important issue in the development of alternative literacy assessment strategies is the whole notion of how children learn to read and write.

Over the last thirty years or so, researchers from around the world have been looking closely at how children develop literacy skills. As a result, a developmental model of literacy learning has emerged. It is based on the model of initial language acquisition (Holdaway 1979).

Young children learning to speak progress through several stages as they experiment, practice, and receive reinforcement for increasingly successful approximations of conventional speech. For example, as children learn to say "mom" or "dad," the words are initially pronounced imperfectly. Nonetheless, adults do not typically respond with didactic criticism. Instead, the child's first approximations of "ma-ma" and "da-da" are rewarded with praise and excitement. Children are consequently encouraged to go on experimenting, practicing, and making more and more sense of the complex world of language.

> If children learn naturally in supportive, reinforcing environments where learning is whole, meaningful, and functional, then the assessment of this learning must be compatible.

Thus the child progresses from sounds to words to sentences. All the while, parents and other adults reinforce and acknowledge the continually improving approximations. Almost all children easily learn to speak and communicate with others in this natural, developmental process. Why then, has reading and writing been taught in such a different way? Why did teachers and researchers believe for so long that instruction for literacy should break learning up into tiny chunks and feed it to children in a controlled, lockstep process?

We now know that literacy learning is very much like initial language acquisition (Clay 1991; Clay 1979; Holdaway 1979). Children progress through stages of literacy learning just as they pass through stages of language acquisition.

Don Holdaway has explored the acquisition of literacy through a natural learning classroom model. It includes the stages of demonstration, participation, performance, and practice/role-play (Fisher 1991). Children begin this natural learning process even before they enter school by observing their parents read and write. In school and at home, children (even those in the earliest stages) are encouraged to demonstrate that they have acquired knowledge about literacy.

Children often begin by scribbling. To them, their scrawls represent names, objects, and lists. These early approximations of conventional writing are reinforced in much the same way that parents reinforce the beginning sounds of "ma-ma" and "da-da." Holdaway's natural learning model continues through the stages with continual and consistent approximation, reinforcement, and celebration in school and at home.

Assessment is not an end, but a means to begin the next stage of learning.

This natural learning model exemplifies many beliefs about how children learn and naturally extends to the development of strategies to assess this learning. If children learn naturally in supportive, reinforcing environments where learning is whole, meaningful, and functional, then the assessment of this learning must be compatible. It must be supportive and reinforcing. It must have purpose and meaningful context, connections to individual learning styles, and implications for classroom instructional practices. With this kind of approach, assessment is not an end, but a means to begin the next stage of learning.

ESSENTIAL COMPONENTS OF PORTFOLIO ASSESSMENT

Portfolios of student work for the purpose of assessment must be flexible. "Flexible," however, does not mean unstructured, spontaneous, or without careful design. In fact, portfolios have to be conceived with a plan in mind. It must provide answers to at least four questions: What needs to be assessed? Who will be involved in the assessment process? How will data be collected and analyzed? What components will be included in the portfolio?

Although it is essential that a portfolio have a component framework, there is no one right way to construct a portfolio, and it is unwise to insist that certain specific elements be included. Rather, teachers must be allowed to consider a wide range of possible portfolio components and to select those that will best reflect the growth and progress of all students, whatever their level of development.

Teachers will need training in the many assessment strategies available if they are to select appropriate portfolio components.

Only if the portfolio assesses a wide range of literacy skills, strategies, and processes can its portrayal of each student be detailed, descriptive, and accurately reflective of student growth and development. The practical implication of this observation is that teachers will need training in the many assessment strategies available if they are to select appropriate portfolio components for individual students or a whole class.

The possible components of a portfolio include:

- observational/anecdotal records
- checklists
- work samples
- formal literacy skill assessments
- informal skill assessments
- student self-assessments
- conference logs and records and

- various types of journals and learning logs.

Since more should be said about each of these components, the rest of this chapter will discuss them one by one.

OBSERVATION AND ANECDOTAL RECORDS

At the heart of assessment lies observation. Observation does not simply mean watching as children work on activities or interact with others. It means watching with the trained and astute eye of someone who knows that everything children say or do has meaning. The skilled observer can tell whether learning has occurred or intervention is needed.

To apply observational skills in portfolio assessment, teachers must document what they see for later reflection and assessment (Fisher 1991). Teachers who observe and record such anecdotal pieces of data in a meaningful way on a regular basis are able to weave a rich picture of a child's daily learning.

This record will also provide data that is useful in instruction, since from the data, teachers can "derive interpretations, value judgments, and evaluations" (Church

> *It means watching with the trained and astute eye of someone who knows that everything children say or do has meaning.*

1991). For example, a teacher observing a group of students working in their journals on a writing workshop exercise might note that several students are having difficulties with a particular vowel pattern or blend. That teacher has collected data that has direct implications for a small-group or whole-class minilesson.

A few suggestions for making the most of anecdotal records in portfolio assessment strategies:

1. *Base observations on activities that use materials and procedures that are interesting to children* (Kemp 1987). The information collected during meaningful and motivating work is likely to be truly reflective of the student's real ability. Observing a child who is bored with an activity will not provide the best data on development.

2. *Focus observational records on both areas of strength and areas in need of development.* Often, teachers tend to focus

on one or the other. Meaningful and useful observations must give equal consideration to both.
3. *Do an on-the-spot preliminary analysis of observations.* In this way, students can be questioned about their strategies, and teachers can make instant revisions in their instructional methods.
4. *Document observations in the course of the instructional process, not at the end of the day.* If observations are to be meaningful later on, they need to show what a child is able to do at that moment, and the record should include specific examples for later analysis.

To make daily notations, some teachers use clipboards with paper grids that have a labeled box for each student. Other teachers write their observations on blank self-adhesive labels or yellow sticky notes, which are placed in a notebook with a section for each student. Another alternative is a spiral-bound book of index cards with several cards allocated to each student. A teacher can keep such a card book in a pocket, jotting down notes as needed.

5. *Make observational and anecdotal records often, and include specific data.* A notation that "Richie had a good day" is meaningless within a day or two. On the other hand, "Richie was able to write the initial sound of "f" for "fireworks" in his journal" or "Today Richie started putting spaces between words in his journal" gives precise evidence of Richie's progress. The more specific entries also give information that assists the teacher in making judgments about how to help Richie to the next stage of literacy development.

CHECKLISTS

A natural extension of collecting daily observational records is the organization of the data into a meaningful whole. The result is a checklist. This synthesis of data is a useful organizational tool for teachers, one that can identify patterns of growth and stages of development.

From research about the stages of literacy learning, and from experience with children over many years, teachers know

Figure 3
Primary Reading/Writing Checklist

An Excerpt from a Primary Reading/Writing Checklist

Name: _____

Grade: _____

U=Usually
S=Sometimes
N=Not yet

Quarters:	1st	2nd	3rd	4th
Shows an interest in books.				
Uses free time to look at books.				
Participates in group reading activities.				
Understands and uses environmental print.				
Displays understanding of letter/sound association.				
Displays understanding of "word."				
Recognizes some words by sight.				
Displays understanding of "story."				
Applies story structures to personal writing.				

that there are several broad categories of growth or "signposts of literacy development"(Church 1991):

- conventions, skills, and mechanics of language
- comprehension and understanding of written and oral language
- language use for a variety of purposes and audiences
- social interactions and problem-solving skills
- attitude and interest toward literacy and
- independent and cooperative work strategies.

Each of these broad categories can be broken down into specific behaviors that teachers can observe, identify, and record on a checklist. This approach allows for the central documentation of progress in a format that teachers, parents, administrators, and students can easily understand. A checklist of literacy indicators also allows the teacher to document progress on the form periodically (quarterly, for example), so that the record will show the time frames when a student first displayed control over a specific behavior. See Figure 3 for an example of a primary reading/writing checklist.

WORK SAMPLES

The old saying that "a picture is worth a thousand words" certainly has its place in the discussion of portfolio assessment. An actual piece of student work can express more detailed data than many other portfolio components.

From the beginning stages of assessment, the teacher and student work together to select the work samples that are most reflective of student progress across a range of literacy behaviors, over time, and with a broad range of genres. In this process, it is very important for students to be helped to make judgments about their work (Graves and Sunstein 1992). It is also important to collect evidence of student work in various stages of completion: first drafts, revisions, and final, "published" work.

An actual piece of student work can express more detailed data than many other portfolio components.

Rather than quickly assembling work in May for a final conference, students and teachers must constantly shuffle the work samples, make judgments about each piece (Graves and Sunstein 1992), and provide a rationale for the inclusion of each piece in the portfolio. This deliberation can be done as simply as scheduling a monthly "portfolio review" with each student. At that time, students and teachers can discuss the portfolio's contents. Dated sticky notes or index cards can be attached to the entries with specific information about the context in which the work was created and the rationale for including particular pieces of work.

There may also be times for teachers to make independent decisions about including certain pieces because they are thought to reflect the acquisition of specific skills or strategies. This evidence of mastery, which may relate directly to items on a literacy checklist, is particularly helpful in that it provides concrete examples of student growth to parents and administrators.

FORMAL LITERACY SKILL ASSESSMENTS

While a great deal of data can be gathered from informal observations, anecdotal records, and work samples, some of the more formal assessments available can provide very specific information about an individual student's literacy development. Such assessments can tell us about specific skill and strategy development in a child's overall concepts about literacy, spelling and phonetic skill development, expressive writing proficiency, and oral reading fluency and comprehension.

The formal assessments provide valuable information that classroom teachers can apply immediately in practice.

Like standardized tests, the formal skill analysis assessments can provide baseline and comparison information, but they can do so within the authentic context of a classroom. In addition, the formal assessments provide valuable information that classroom teachers can apply immediately in practice.

Concepts About Literacy

When young children enter school, they have already had experiences with print. Most children can recognize a McDonald's restaurant sign and can often pick out the name of their favorite cereal at the grocery store. From early experiences at home, most young children also know what books are and that they contain information that can be read. Tots often memorize stories and know when a parent skips part of a favorite story.

When formal schooling begins, it is often helpful for teachers to make formal records of these early understandings about print and books. The results will alert teachers about children who have not had these early experiences with print and text. The findings will also comprise baseline data, so that when assessments are readministered later in the year, comparisons can be made.

The assessments of early conceptual understanding include:

1. *CAP or Concepts About Print* (Clay 1991; Clay 1979). This early literacy assessment, developed in 1972 by Marie Clay, covers a broad range of early reading behaviors. The assessment is quite valuable for nonreaders and emerging readers alike. It is especially useful "to reflect changes in reading skill during the first year of instruction, but is of less significance in the later years" (Clay 1979). Clay has used the assessment to identify age ranges within which children should have mastered specific concepts.

   CAP requires the use of a specific storybook designed expressly for this assessment. The 24-part assessment begins with simple items that ask the child to identify the front of the book and the message in print. Then items increase in complexity. The child is asked to notice irregularities in the print, various punctuation markings, and eventually, single letters and words. Teachers record responses on a specific data sheet, and make comments as appropriate about the child's behavior.

2. *Print and Book Knowledge* (Kemp 1987). This assessment is similar to *Concepts About Print,* but with a couple of significant differences. First, the assessment can be used with any age or grade level since its questions cover a wider range of

reading skills and behaviors than *Concepts About Print* does. Second, *Print and Book Knowledge* allows the teacher to conduct the assessment with a book from the classroom collection, so long as the book chosen is a fairly close match with the child's reading level.

During the assessment, the teacher gives the child the book and asks a series of questions dealing with both conceptual understandings and specific letter and word recognition skills. The first simple questions ask about the front cover, the title, and the first page. Then, increasingly complex questions ask about sentences, letters, punctuation, paragraphs, and so on. Teachers make notations about the child's responses. Naturally, the assessment can be readministered to compare knowledge over time.

> *The assessment can be readministered to compare knowledge over time.*

3. *Sulzby Storybook Classification Scheme* (Valencia and Sulzby 1991). This assessment is based on the notion that "children emergently acquire all aspects of conventional literacy and that they reorganize these aspects into a coordinated, flexible, integrated system, which allows them to figure out print independently" (Valencia and Sulzby 1991).

This scheme, designed to be used with familiar storybooks, consists of a set of descriptions with 11 subcategories of reading behaviors from emergent to independent. The child is asked to "read" the book, and the teacher listens and keeps records of how the child proceeds. The behaviors observed are then compared to the classification scheme and developmental levels of reading.

Spelling and Phonetic Skill Development

As young children in a natural environment represent sounds and words, their responses give clues as to how the children understand letter-to-sound associations. Formal assessments can be used to document the young writer's ability to represent sounds in conventional spelling. Such assessments involve student-generated lists of words and teacher-dictated words and passages.

1. *Clay Procedure* (Kemp 1987). This assessment of a child's first attempts at independent writing provides important data on the conventions of spelling that a child has internalized and can use independently, as opposed to the conventions that the child needs reinforcement on or has not yet been exposed to.

   In the procedure, which can be done several times throughout the year, the child is instructed to write as many words as he or she can within ten minutes. If the child is unable to begin, the teacher may say something like "Can you write your name?" or "Do you know any little words, like 'Mom,' or 'Dad,' or 'I'"?

   After ten minutes, the child reads the words back to the teacher. Children are given one point for each word they write correctly. Points are deducted for a word read as something else, even if the word is accurate as written. More important than the actual point total, however, are the observations that a teacher makes as the child is writing (Kemp 1987).

2. *Dictation Analysis.* This procedure, also developed by Clay, is based on passage dictation and a child's ability to make connections between "known phoneme and grapheme relationships" (Kemp 1987). With the information gathered from this assessment, the teacher is able to detect a child's process of encoding the spoken word into written form, along with specific spelling and phonics areas that need reinforcement. The assessment can be done many times throughout the year with individuals or an entire class. The actual passages dictated may be derived from classroom texts or developed by groups of teachers.

   The teacher dictates one of several passages to a child, who must independently encode the orally presented sentence. Each graphophonic unit is considered as one (in other words, the "ing" phoneme would be counted as one sound because the three letters make a single sound). A child receives one point for each unit correctly encoded. The number of points a child receives for correctly written units is divided by the total number of units in the

$$\frac{\text{Correctly written units}}{\text{total \# of units}} \times 100 = \text{score (\%)}$$

entire passage. The result is multiplied times 100 to generate a percentage score.

For example, the teacher might dictate the following passage (Kemp 1987):

> . . . .
> "My mom goes to work. She brings me to school in the car."

This passage contains 33 graphophonemic units, which are indicated by the dots over each unit.

Suppose, then, that a child encodes the passage this way:

> . X . . . . X. . . . X. . . . . X . . . . . . X. X
> Mi mom gos to wrk. She brngs me to skool in the cr.

The child receives one point for each unit encoded correctly (each dot represents one point each; x represents one point missed). In all, the child received 27 of 33 possible points, which computes to a score of 82 percent.

Expressive Writing Proficiency

As children progress through developmental stages in spelling and phonetic skill development, their spontaneous and expressive writing skills are also progressing. To document both the student's evolving control over conventions and advances in the processes of expressive writing, the teacher can periodically analyze a portion of a student's writing (Kemp 1987). These analyses can be used to make comparisons over months and years.

The teacher begins the analysis by selecting a portion of expressive writing that a child has worked on independently as a first draft. A selection of approximately 50 words is adequate. The teacher then proceeds through the following steps:

1. Determine the "total vocabulary" by counting the number of words that are not repeated (for example, if the student uses the word "the" five times, count it only once) (Kemp 1987).

2. Underline and count the words that have been written incorrectly. Subtract this number from the total vocabulary. The resulting number of words written correctly is the "words stabilized" figure (Kemp 1987).

3. Divide the words stabilized figure by the total vocabulary figure and multiply the result times 100 to generate a percentage.
4. Document the exact errors on a tally sheet and attach it to the original of the student's work. This record provides qualitative data on word patterns that may be troublesome or on words that may need reinforcement. Keeping the original of the student's work also provides insight into the development of personal style and voice and the student's facility with vocabulary and conventions.

Oral Reading Fluency and Comprehension

By performing a miscue analysis at key points in a child's early reading development, a teacher can collect critical data on oral reading, the use of reading strategies, comprehension, and the overall development of the reading process (Kemp 1987). Two different types of miscue analysis can be done. In one, the teacher pays close attention to a word-by-word oral reading. The other concentrates on a sentence-by-sentence oral reading.

> *The response provides insight into comprehension, sequence, and the understanding of story structure.*

1. *Word Miscue.* For this type of analysis, the teacher needs several passages on increasing levels of difficulty and complexity. The teacher asks each child to read one or more passages on the child's reading level. On a copy of the passage being read, the teacher makes detailed notes that indicate errors, such as when words or passages are repeated, read incorrectly, or omitted altogether. Teachers can develop their own shorthand for these notations or may use systems suggested in resources on miscue analysis (Valencia 1990a; Kemp 1987; Clay 1979).

   Once the child completes the passage, the teacher may ask the child to summarize the passage. The response provides insight into comprehension, sequence, and the understanding of story structure.

   Each child's reading is audiotaped. The tape is later used for a careful analysis of the child's oral reading. The teacher counts the total number of errors made (not counting self-corrections) and subtracts these miscue errors from the total word count. The number of words read correctly is divided by the total word count of the passage and multiplied by 100 to yield a percentage. This figure, which represents the accuracy rate for each child's oral reading, should be greater than 90 percent if the child is to be considered an independent reader at a particular level.

2. *Sentence Miscue* (Valencia 1990a). This method (also called the *Classroom Miscue Reading Assessment*) concentrates on the accurate reading of each sentence in a passage, rather than on each word. The main interest is to see if children make sense of what they are reading, so they are given credit for each semantically acceptable sentence read. If, for example, a child reads a sentence and substitutes the word "home" for "house," the performance is considered semantically acceptable because the sentence still makes sense. If the child reads "hose" instead of "house," however, the sentence would be semantically unacceptable, and it would be scored as incorrect.

For each passage read, the number of semantically acceptable sentences is divided by the total number of sentences read, and the result is multiplied by 100 to generate a percentage "comprehension score." Proficient readers score at approximately 80 percent or above, 60 to 80 percent is average, and below 60 percent is considered poor (Valencia 1990a).

Both types of miscue analysis provide similar information, but sentence miscue is a quicker screening method, while word miscue provides a more precise analysis of specific phonetic and syntactic characteristics. Classroom teachers must decide which approach is most appropriate for their students. Both can be useful tools in the analysis and documentation of reading progress in young students.

STUDENT SELF-ASSESSMENTS

As students display increasing control over their reading skills and strategies, teachers should involve them in the assessment process, since the information that students provide can be extremely revealing. Self-assessment does not happen automatically, however, so teachers must provide the means and mechanisms for self-assessments to become an integral part of student portfolios. Students need frequent opportunities "to monitor, reflect upon, and evaluate their own progress, learning strategies, work habits, products, and achievements. Self-evaluation should be a key activity in every classroom" (Anthony et al. 1991).

> *Self-assessment does not happen automatically. Students need frequent opportunities to monitor, reflect upon, and evaluate their own progress.*

The means through which self-evaluation can be incorporated into portfolio assessment include learning logs, survey questions, and student selection of portfolio entries.

Learning Logs

Learning logs are a special kind of notebook intended "to encourage self-monitoring and reflection" (Anthony et al. 1991). In the logs, students periodically record observations, feelings, insights, and judgments about their work and themselves as learners. As children come to feel comfortable with the process, they may be encouraged to share their logs with friends.

Very young students can dictate their thoughts to teachers or volunteers who actually do the writing in the logs. Later on, prompts can be effective in helping children get started. Some prompts, for example, are:

- The best thing about this activity was . . .
- I didn't like . . . because . . .
- It was hard for me when I had to . . .

Survey Questions

Students at all ages can respond to survey-type questions about specific activities, projects, or their learning in general. To indicate likes, dislikes, and feelings, young children can draw "happy faces" or "sad faces" to answer questions that the teacher reads aloud.

Student Selection of Portfolio Entries

Students need opportunities to select pieces of work to be included in the portfolios and then to reflect on the choices made. A small paper attached to each selection can provide extremely valuable information and insight into a child's thoughts and processes. The papers attached may have prompts like:

- I selected this piece because . . .
- This piece shows that I am able to . . .
- This work shows that I need to work more on . . .

This kind of information leads directly to individualized goal setting between the student and teacher. It also encourages students to take increased responsibility for their own learning.

CONFERENCES

When teachers think of conferences, the image that generally comes to mind is parents and a teacher meeting together to discuss a child's work and progress. Conferences have come a long way, though, and they now may include students and peers in addition to parents. Any or all of such conferences can provide a very effective way for students, teachers, and parents to reflect on progress made and to set appropriate goals for the future.

Conferences with Students

Many teachers have found that meeting individually with children to hear them read or to discuss their writing can be richly rewarding (Johnson and Louis 1990). Together the teacher and student can discuss revisions that were made or may need to be made in written work, strategies that proved particularly effective for the student, and evidence of growth and progress in the work at hand.

Documentation of student-teacher conferences can take many forms. Some teachers use checklists of reading and writing skills, and a record is made of the ones that were either attempted or used well (Johnson and Louis 1990). Other teachers make notes on index cards and attach them to work in progress. Still others keep a log in each child's portfolio or folder and make brief notations during or after each conference so that, in future work, students can refer back to the conference notes and use the information discussed. Naturally, teachers may also create their own conference documentation form to sum up formal or informal conferences.

Conferences with Peers

Within this framework, students meet with each other periodically to share written work or to read books together (paired groupings are usually the most effective). While one student takes a turn, the other listens and responds.

For these types of conferences to be effective, the classroom teacher must spend time teaching students how to confer. Students need to learn about appropriate questioning techniques and how to give constructive comments and suggestions (Tierney, Carter, and Desai 1991).

Thus, prior to the peer conferences, the teacher must model appropriate listening and responding behaviors. Teachers who make this time investment, however, will get valuable dividends. When students learn how to be good peer coaches, the technique is usually very successful. These students are able to listen attentively to their peers and respond with specific comments and suggestions in relation to the work or the passage read. They may make suggestion concerning story structure, sequencing, or character development in a student's written work, or about expression and fluency after a reading task. Perhaps most importantly, peer coaches praise and encourage developing readers and writers while learning to value each other's efforts.

Conferences with Parents

The inclusion of parents in the overall assessment process is critically important. They need to be involved in more than just the final stage of the process if they are to see all the skills and strategies that their children are developing and to assist their children along the way.

Parent involvement with portfolios can take many forms, including holding three-way conferences that include students, teachers, and parents. Parents may also respond in writing to the work in the portfolio. They can complete a questionnaire about their perceptions of the student's work and provide examples that the parent thinks is indicative of growth. Having such comments in writing is motivating to students.

LOGS AND JOURNALS

Many teachers and researchers have discussed the powerful role that logs and journals can have in the assessment process (Donohoe 1992; Graves and Sunstein 1992; Goodman and Hood 1989; Milz 1990; Tierney, Carter, and Desai 1991). These logs and journals probably have as many forms as there are teachers who use them. Among the many types, are:

- student logs of books read and a brief "review" of the book
- logs of strategies and conventions displayed in written work or oral reading, along with the frequency of use
- logs of conferences with teachers, peers, and parents
- updates on works in progress and works completed
- responses to classroom lessons and activities
- students' personal responses to independent reading
- home-school journals discussing activities and progress, and
- expressive writing or diaries of students' personal reflections.

The possible variations of logs and journals is truly endless. Teachers can adapt these learning tools in many, many ways.

Teachers use logs and journals frequently because of their power to aid student reflection and document growth. For instance, students and teachers may be able to see at a glance the books that have been read or the skills that have been mastered in written work. Such information provides invaluable qualitative and quantitative data and therefore deserves an important place in the assessment process.

Portfolios are dynamic, fluid mechanisms for the assessment of student progress and development and are not stagnant receptacles or simple files of student work. Teachers and students need to work together to select those components that reflect the ranges of development through a broad and complete representation.

# PUTTING PORTFOLIO ASSESSMENT TO WORK

CREATING AN ENVIRONMENT THAT SUPPORTS PORTFOLIO ASSESSMENT

The classroom environment includes factors such as the role of the classroom teacher, the arrangement of the daily routine, and the physical layout of the classroom space. You can manipulate these factors to suport your portfolio assessment process.

The Role of the Classroom Teacher

The philosophy of the classroom teacher is perhaps the most important aspect of a classroom environment that supports portfolio assessment in both its theoretical and practical aspects. Teachers need to see themselves as participants and facilitators rather than managers or directors (Milz 1990). It is the responsibility of teachers to gather materials and create environments that support young language learners in all respects.

Portfolios are dynamic, fluid assessment mechanisms.

Teachers must also continually model behavior that respects individuality, team effort, the value of contributions from all learners, and the importance of continuous learning and growth. Likewise, teachers not only need to model strategies for reading and writing, but also can make a vital contribution by modeling appropriate behavior when they make mistakes!

When teachers make mistakes in front of children, and then talk through their strategies for correcting the problem, students are provided with strategies that they can incorporate into their own learning processes. Students see that making mistakes and learning to correct them is a part of learning and not just something to be avoided.

As teachers begin to incorporate portfolio assessment into practice, they will soon notice changes. The classroom becomes a more dynamic, exciting place where continuous learning can occur. Further, students and the teacher become more reflective and self-aware of their learning and their progress (Voss 1992).

The Arrangement of the Daily Routine

In a classroom community that supports portfolio assessment, the instructional and assessment processes are inseparable, and the two are interactive and collaborative in character (Tierney, Carter, and Desai 1991). An implication is that the daily schedule of the class must be developed to support daily assessment. In other words, time must be allowed for whole-class lessons, small-group work, individual student-teacher conferences, and peer coaching.

Teachers have the responsibility to design a flexible, yet structured, class schedule. These dual goals may seem contradictory, but they are not. In fact, the teacher must walk the line between providing opportunities for individual work and reflection and providing students with instructional opportunities based on the daily assessment of individuals and the class.

It is this balance between structure and flexibility that allows the teacher to engage in daily assessment opportunities with individual and small groups. While children are engaged in producing and reflecting on their work, the teacher may hold formal or informal conferences with students about progress with written work or journals. The teacher may also use the available time to work with individual students or use some type of assessment technique.

> *Teachers have the responsibility to design a flexible, yet structured, class schedule.*

Time is not neatly divided, however, into exclusively instructional and assessment activities. Throughout the day, the teacher is continually assessing and collecting data, perhaps with formalized observational recording techniques, but just as likely, with simple mental notes.

The Physical Layout of the Classroom

All primary teachers know that their classroom must be warm, welcoming, and friendly. A physical environment that supports reflection, self-evaluation, and authentic assessment, however, needs several additional key features (Wortman and Hausslen 1989):

- centers for individual and small-group work around specific activities, for instance, writing centers, math centers, and reading corners
- cubbies for each child to store work in varying stages of completion
- mailboxes that encourage correspondence between students and teachers
- student work folders that are easily accessible to both students and teachers
- access to a variety of writing and materials and books on varying ability levels, and
- a print-rich environment that includes posters and charts of meaningful stories and lists of words and names (Routman 1988).

INTERPRETING AND ANALYZING PORTFOLIOS

As teachers and students collect work for portfolios, reflect on which pieces to include, conduct formal and informal assessments, and confer about growth and progress, teachers may ask, What now? What do I do with all of this information? And how do I use it to understand my students better?

The interpretation of portfolios is truly an art rather than a science. Teachers can gather quantitative and qualitative data in many areas, but without careful, reflective interpretation and analysis, the data is nothing more than files of student work. The careful interpretation of portfolios takes time and effort. As part of the analytical process, students need to spend time looking back over past works and drawing conclusions about their own growth. Teachers need to spend time with colleagues looking at student work and discussing the implications of it. Teachers also need to think about how the information drawn from student work samples can be incorporated into daily instructional practices.

> *Teachers can gather quantitative and qualitative data in many areas, but without careful, reflective interpretation and analysis, the data is nothing more than files of student work.*

In the course of discussions about student portfolios, some important questions for teachers to keep in mind are:

- What do these work samples indicate about the student's developmental level in reading and writing?
- In view of past works, how has the student progressed, and is this progress developmentally appropriate?
- Which pieces has the student self-selected, and why?
- What areas are evident as strengths, and which seem to be in need of further reinforcement?
- From the data gathered, what are the instructional implications, both for individual students and for the class as a whole?
- On the basis of the data collected, what goals seem appropriate for individuals and for the class?

Of course, teachers may ask many other questions based on their individual experiences and the experiences of their classes. Always, bear in mind the fluid nature of portfolios as an assessment process.

COMMUNICATING STUDENT GROWTH AND DEVELOPMENT TO PARENTS

Many of today's parents are not fully aware of rapidly developing educational reforms. Parents want the best for their children, yet often don't understand new methods and strategies in education. Thinking back to their own experiences with school, parents hear "assessment" and immediately think "tests."

It is up to teachers and administrators to share the extensive benefits of portfolio assessment with today's parents. This interchange of ideas and methods needs to be done early in the school year, so that parents understand how their child's progress will be tracked and assessed and how the parents will be kept informed.

Teachers and administrators have a responsibility to share the extensive benefits of portfolio assessment with today's parents.

Figure 4
Keeping Parents in the Loop: A Checklist

☐ Early letter to parents about portfolio practices.
  - Identify classes (or entire school) that will be using portfolio assessment
  - Send home articles and research that show the benefits of portfolio assessment
  - Be cognizant of potential language barriers for non-English-speaking parents

☐ Send parents detailed information on portfolio components.

☐ Have a mock portfolio available to show parents who "drop by" the school.

☐ Provide an early opportunity for parents to meet with teachers to discuss portfolios and how teachers will interpret the data collected.

☐ Give parents an opportunity to select work or provide other portfolio components.

☐ For parent conferences, review each portfolio component and all work samples:
  - Explain what each piece tells about their child's progress.
  - Highlight areas of strength
  - Point out areas where parents can help with reinforcement
  - Work with parents to set goals

☐ Give parents option to view and comment on the portfolios periodically.

Portfolio assessment generally represents change or modification from past practices. To effect such a major change in the smoothest, most positive manner possible, teachers and administrators might consider these recommendations:

- Inform parents early that a particular class, or an entire school, is using portfolio assessment practices. Explain exactly what this system entails, either through newsletters or a parent information night. Provide articles and research as evidence of the many benefits of this method and of successful implementations of portfolios in other schools (Fisher 1991).

- Give parents detailed information about the components that are being incorporated into the portfolios. Perhaps even show a mock portfolio with several typical items that could be included.

- Early in the school year, provide opportunities for parents to meet with the teacher to discuss what portfolios look like in specific classrooms and how the teacher interprets the data collected.

- During parent conferences, review each of the portfolio components and work samples. Explain exactly what each piece tells in terms of progress, areas of strength, areas in need of reinforcement, and goals to be set.

- Give parents the option to comment periodically on the portfolios, either at conference times or other times throughout the year.

Once mothers and fathers see samples of their child's work, accounts of the books they've read, and other concrete examples of the progress that has been made, the parents are likely to be quite impressed and supportive of portfolios as a means of assessment.

TAKING THE FIRST STEPS TOWARD PORTFOLIO ASSESSMENT

Teachers who are intrigued by portfolio assessment strategies and techniques should not be overwhelmed by their breadth or depth. Because portfolios are so fluid and flexible, teachers can begin using portfolio assessment in small steps. The entire classroom does not have to be overhauled overnight! In fact, teachers should proceed with small, effective steps that allow for reflection and revision as needed over time.

> *Teachers should proceed with small, effective steps.*

For teachers just beginning to investigate portfolio assessment techniques and strategies, the following tips may be helpful:

1. Make preliminary decisions about how the portfolio system will work in your classroom. For example, will student work folders feed into a "master portfolio" kept by the teacher? How will the system be described to the class? In the beginning, what will the role of students be? (It is probably best to start slowly and build to more complex organizational strategies later.)

2. Gather materials, such as folders, binders, and other materials for record-keeping strategies. Set aside a place for students to keep their folders and for the safekeeping of master portfolios.

3. Become familiar with the techniques and formal procedures that will be used as portfolio components.

4. Collect some student work samples, dating everything and making notes about the context of the work. As students come to an understanding of the process, have them participate in selecting and weeding out samples over the course of the school year.

5. Begin collecting daily observational and anecdotal records. Instead of focusing on every child every day, try alternatives. For example, select three or four children each day and rotate, so that by the end of two weeks, all children have been observed in detail.

6. Begin to use some formalized data collection techniques. This initiative can begin as simply as having all children write a two- or three-sentence dictated passage that is subsequently analyzed and kept in the portfolio. The same sentences could be dictated in four weeks to permit comparison and the assessment of progress.

As both formal and informal data collection continues, take time out every other week or so to look over the student portfolios. Look for trends in skill and strategy development. Make notes about specific students or about the class as a whole. This work will begin to hone your interpretative and analytical skills concerning portfolio components. The most important interpretive skill, however, is listening and learning from the students. Everything they do and every piece of work in their portfolios tells a piece of the child's story. Each piece of data should be treated as a golden nugget of information leading to greater insight into the development and progress of a child.

> *The most important interpretive skill is listening and learning from the students.*

BIBLIOGRAPHY

Anthony, R. J.; Johnson, T. P.; Mickelson, N. I; and Preece, A. *Evaluating Literacy.* Portsmouth, N. H.: Heinemann Publications, 1991.

Arter, J. A., and Spandel, V. "Using Portfolios of Student Work in Instruction and Assessment." *Educational Measurement: Issues and Practices* 11, no. 1 (1992): 36-44.

Balm, S.S. "Using Portfolio Assessment in a Kindergarten Classroom." *Teaching and Change* 2, no. 2 (1995): 141-51.

Baron, J. B. "Performance Assessment: Blurring the Edges Among Assessment, Curriculum, and Instruction." *This Year in School Science, 1990: Assessment in the Service of Instruction.* American Association for the Advancement of Science, 1990.

Berlak, H. "The Need for a New Science of Assessment." In *Toward a New Science of Education and Assessment.* Albany, N.Y.: State University of New York Press, 1992.

California Learning Record. Sacramento, Calif.: California Department of Public Instruction, 1992.

Carstens, L. *The California Learning Record.* Report prepared for the San Diego City Schools: March 10, 1992.

Chittenden, E. "Authentic Assessment, Evaluation, and Documentation of Student Performance." In *Expanding Student Assessment,* edited by V. Perrone. Alexandria, Va.: Association for Supervision and Curriculum Development, 1991.

Church, C. J. "Record Keeping in Whole Language Classrooms." In *Assessment and Evaluation in Whole Language Programs,* edited by B. Harp. Norwood, Mass.: Christopher-Gordon Publishers, 1991.

Clay, M. *Becoming Literate.* Portsmouth, N. H.: Heinemann Publications, 1991.

———. *The Early Detection of Reading Difficulties.* Portsmouth, N. H.: Heinemann Publications, 1979.

Donahoe, C. G. "Home-School Journals: Reflections that Connect Students, Parents, and Teachers." *California Assessment Collaborative Newsletter* 2, no. 1 (1992).

Elbow, P. "Foreword." In *Portfolios: Process and Product,* edited by P. Belanoff and M. Dickson. Portsmouth, N. H.: Heinemann Publications, 1991.

Farr, R. "Putting It All Together: Solving the Reading Assessment Puzzle." *The Reading Teacher* 46, no.1 (1992): 26-29.

Fisher, B. *Joyful Learning.* Portsmouth, N. H.: Heinemann Publications, 1991.

Flood, J., and Lapp, D. "Reporting Reading Progress: A Comparison Portfolio for Parents." *The Reading Teacher* 43, no. 7 (1989): 508-14.

Frederiksen, J. R., and Collins, A. "A Systems Approach to Educational Testing." *Educational Researcher* 18, no. 9 (1989): 27-32.

French, R. L. "Portfolio Assessment and LEP Students." *Focus on Evaluation and Measurement* 1 and 2. Proceedings of the National Research Symposium on Limited English Proficient Student Issues, Washington, D.C., September 1991.

Glazer, S. M., and Brown, C. S. *Portfolios and Beyond.* Norwood, Mass.: Christopher-Gordon Publishers, 1993.

Goodman, K. S.; Goodman, Y.; and Hood, W. J., eds. *The Whole Language Evaluation Book.* Portsmouth, N. H.: Heinemann Publications, 1989.

Graves, D. H., and Sunstein, B. S. *Portfolio Portraits.* Portsmouth, N. H.: Heinemann Publications, 1992.

Grovenor, L. et al. *Student Portfolios.* Washington, D.C.: National Education Association, NEA Teacher-to-Teacher Books, 1993.

Haney, W. "We Must Take Care: Fitting Assessments to Functions." In *Expanding Student Assessment,* edited by V. Perrone. Alexandria, Va.: Association for Supervision and Curriculum Development, 1991.

Harp, B. "Principles of Assessment and Evaluation in Whole Language Classrooms." In *Assessment and Evaluation in Whole Language Programs.* Norwood, Mass.: Christopher-Gordon Publishers, 1991.

Holdaway, D. *The Foundations of Literacy.* Portsmouth, N. H.: Heinemann Publications, 1979.

Hornsby, D., and Sukarna, D. *Read On: The Conference Approach to Reading.* Portsmouth, N. H.: Heinemann Publications, 1988.

Johnson, T. D., and Louis, D. R. *Bringing It All Together: A Program for Literacy.* Portsmouth, N. H.: Heinemann Publications, 1990.

Jongsma, K. S. "Portfolio Assessment." *The Reading Teacher* 44, no. 3 (1989): 264-65.

Kemp, M. *Watching Children Read and Write.* Portsmouth, N. H.: Heinemann Publications, 1987.

Linek, W. M. "Grading and Evaluation Techniques for Whole Language Teachers." *Language Arts* 68 (February 1991): 125-32.

Linn, R. L.; Baker, E. L.; and Dunbar, S. B. "Complex Performance-Based Assessment: Expectations and Validation Criteria." *Educational Researcher* (November 1991): 15-21.

Lyman. L.; Foyle, H. C.; and Azwell, T. S. "Assessing Cooperative Learning Through Portfolios." In *Cooperative Learning in the Elementary Classroom.* Washington, D.C.: National Education Association, 1993.

Maeroff, G. I. "Assessing Alternative Assessment." *Phi Delta Kappan* 73, no. 4 (1991): 272-81.

Milz, V. E. "Supporting Literacy Development: On the First Day in First Grade and Throughout the Year." In *Portraits of Whole Language Classrooms,* edited by H. Mills and J. A. Clyde. Portsmouth, N. H.: Heinemann Publications, 1990.

Mitchell, R. "Testing for Learning." In *Perspective: Council For Basic Education* 4, no. 2 (1992): 1-6

National Education Association. *Assessing Learning in the Classroom.* Washington, D.C.: National Education Association, 1994.

Newman, C. and Smolen, L. "Portfolio Assessment in Our Schools: Implementation, Advantages, and Concerns." *Midwestern Educational Researcher* 6, no.1 (1993): 28-32.

Nweke, W. C. "What Type of Evidence Is Provided through the Portfolio Assessment Method?" Paper presented at the annual meeting of the Mid-South Educational Research Association, Lexington, Ky. November 1991.

Reardon, S. J. "A Collage of Assessment and Evaluation in Primary Grade Classrooms." In *Assessment and Evaluation in Whole Language Programs,* edited by B. Harp. Portsmouth, N. H.: Heinemann Publications, 1991.

Routman, R. *Transitions: From Literature to Literacy.* Portsmouth, N. H.: Heinemann Publications, 1988.

Ryan, C. W. "Authentic Assessment of Self-Concept through Portfolios: Building a Model with Public Schools." Paper presented at the annual meeting of the American Association of Colleges for Teacher Education, Chicago, Ill, February 1994.

Searfoss, L. W. "Assessing Classroom Environments." In *Portfolios and Beyond,* edited by S. M. Glazer and C. S. Brown. Norwood, Mass.: Christopher-Gordon Publishers, 1993.

Silvernail, D. L. "Alternative Forms of Student Assessment: Establishing their Validity." *Journal of Maine Education* 8, no. 1 (1992): 27-31.

Stiggins, R. J. "Assessment Literacy." *Phi Delta Kappan* (March 1991): 534-39.

Stock, P. L. "The Rhetoric of Writing Assessment." In *Expanding Student Assessment,* edited by V. Perrone. Alexandria, Va.: Association for Supervision and Curriculum Development, 1991.

Teale, W. H. "Developmentally Appropriate Assessment of Reading and Writing in the Early Childhood Classroom." *The Elementary School Journal* 89, no. 2 (1988): 173-83.

Tierney, R. J.; Carter, M.; and Desai, L. *Portfolio Assessment in the Reading-Writing Classroom.* Norwood, Mass.: Christopher-Gordon Publishers, 1991.

Valencia, S. "Miscue Analysis in the Classroom." *The Reading Teacher* 44, no. 3 (1990a): 252-54.

―――. "A Portfolio Approach to Classroom Reading Assessment." *The Reading Teacher* 43, no. 5 (1990b): 338-40.

Valencia, S., and Sulzby, E. "Assessment of Emergent Literacy: Storybook Reading." *The Reading Teacher* 44, no. 7 (March 1991): 498-500.

Voss, M. M. "Portfolios in First Grade: A Teacher's Discoveries." In *Portfolio Portraits,* edited by D. Graves. Portsmouth, N. H.: Heinemann Publications, 1992.

Winograd, P.; Paris, S.; and Bridge, C. "Improving the Assessment of Literacy." *The Reading Teacher* 45, no. 2 (1991): 108-16.

Wolf, D. P.; Le Mahieu, P. G.; and Eresh, J. "Good Measure: Assessment as a Tool for Educational Reform." *Educational Leadership* 49, no. 8 (1992): 8-13.

Wortman, R., and Hausslen, M. M. "Evaluation in a Classroom Environment Designed for Whole Language." In *The Whole Language Evaluation Book,* edited by K. Goodman. Portsmouth, N. H.: Heinemann Publications, 1989.

Zessoules, R., and Gardner, H. "Authentic Assessment: Beyond the Buzzword and Into the Classroom." In *Expanding Student Assessment,* edited by V. Perrone. Alexandria, Va.: Association for Supervision and Curriculum Development, 1991.